Everyone has a path that leads them through life.
That path is 100% unique to them.
My path has been nothing but straight or easy to navigate.
I have turned to writing to cope and to process.
So here is the journey of my life.
Through My Eyes.

About the Book

In my 20 years on this planet I have experienced:
Loss
Heartbreak
Change
Love
Happiness
Hate
And here is me navigating it all.

About the Author

Written By : Violet Autumn
Cover Art Design By : Yarrow Batiste
Illustrations by : Carina Lopez

Contributors

Love

I look over at you
Eyes still closed softly and if only you knew
I see my future in the depths of your eyes
I watch our life play out and as the time flies
I see all of our moments and smile watching our firsts
Tear up as i hear the words for better or for worse
I can feel the gentleness of your touch on my skin
And the butterflies in my stomach churn from within
Because with you i feel something i've never felt before
Like a little kid walking into the biggest candy store
I love every inch of you, your perfections and your flaws
And if i could i'd freeze this moment by simply pressing pause
There's a warmth to your lips pressing against mine
Your hand touching my cheek sends chills down my spine
I will never grow tired of being here with you
For every moment is magical and i believe it to be true

My Future, Your eyes

My mama taught me
Love them anyways
Care for them always
Hate is exhausting
and love always stays
Darkness is temporary
God lights the way
Laughters the best medicine
True friends won't betray
Family is forever
And life is your runway

Mother knows best

I miss when i was young
When snow days existed and my biggest worry was catching snowflakes on
my tongue
I miss when my mom would sing me to sleep
When the words "can you tickle my back" were said on repeat
I miss when my dad would push us on the swing
Underdogs were the highest currency "again, again, one more time" we would
sing
I miss when we invented games to play
When tickle monster was a nightly occurrence at the end of every day
I miss butterfly and eskimo kisses goodnight
My mom and dad never failing to tuck me in tight
I miss dancing to disney's sing-along-songs
Believing that i can go the distance and one day i'll be right where i belong
I miss the magic of christmas morning
And being pushed into the pool without a single warning
I miss family dinners and sitting at the same table
Being encouraged to try everything and knowing i'll be caught if ever
unstable
I miss whip cream on waffles and breakfast for dinner
Post-competition celebratory meals gotta celebrate the winner
I miss bike riding to starbucks and cold stone in the summer
Being told constantly by my dad that i'm beautiful, quite the stunner
I miss fighting with my siblings over the dumbest of things
Even moving around colorado all the way down to the springs
I miss having my family physically by my side every step of the way
Being told that life is a round of golf and sometimes you're not always in the
fairway
But despite everything that i miss and wish i could return to
The saying you never know you're living the good old days until you're out of
them is true
But the past has prepared us for the future no matter what it is
And sometimes the real tickle monster will emerge and try to shake up life's
bliss
But i have an army behind me no matter how far
They're always there to help me even if it's not to open up the pickle jar
But family is forever
And these memories walk with us through life, hand in hand together

I miss

What do I picture when I picture us?
I picture dancing in the headlights late at night
Getting lost in conversation until darkness breaks to daylight
I picture kisses in the rain
Standing on a hotel balcony, laughing, and popping
champagne
I picture singing our favorite songs into an invisible
microphone
Jamming out to disney music and screaming "into the
unknown"
I picture coffee in bed before long days at work
Texting you from across the room just to see your little smirk
I picture face masks and romcoms, spa days and foot rubs
After long, hard days coming home to your warm hugs
I picture laughing for hours at things only we understand
Walking the boardwalk at sunrise hand in hand
I picture cuddling for hours and talks fantasizing about our life
together
Enjoying the sun but also knowing we can withstand any
weather
I picture inside jokes that only we know
And watching as our connection and love for each other grows
I picture forever when i picture us
And i know we'll get there because in our love i trust

Picture

My vision is blurred from the tears in my eyes
But i won't let a tear fall for nobody deserves to make me cry
Instead i will wait until im alone in my room
To allow the emotions to flood in and the darkness to consume
I am falling in love with someone who is pulling away
And i am familiar with this pattern as nobody tends to stay
But the seat in their back pocket fits me so well
I'm there when they want me at the ring of their bell
And deep down i know that i deserve so much more
But the devil on my shoulder insists loving me is a chore

Loving is a chore

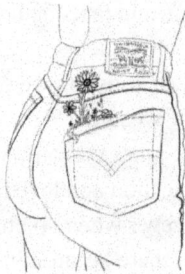

A part of you loves me
And it has taken this long for even me to see
But we have crossed the lines
Into loves territory
And it's a terrifying, yet exhilarating love story

Loves territory

I want to feel your whisper in my ear
Your gentle voice saying exactly what i want to hear
I want to feel your touch on every ounce of my skin
Your soft lips making butterflies churn from within
I want your gentle force to take my breath away
Your embrace to ensure me you are here and here to stay
I want to stare into your coffee brown eyes
Where every star aligns and all emotion lies
I want to feel your breath brush against me
Chills forming in its wake making every part of me plea
For me to have you, all of you, down to every ounce
I am yours and you are mine an easy statement to announce

Want

I find perfection in all of your flaws
Each inch of your being is easy to applaud
I want to know that forever lies with you
Stare into your eyes, smile, and say i do
Hold your hand while we walk through life's rocky road
support if we stumble and need a second to reload
Laugh through our mistakes cause life isn't supposed to be all
serious
Explore the world together enjoy each knew experience
I just want you to want me too
Cause my love for you is not something i can ever undo

Undo

I like you
Not as a friend
Not as a hookup buddy
Not as a trend
Or someone to help study
The kind of like that goes from one to two
Or where liking turns into falling in love with you

Liking to falling

I get lost in those eyes of blue
The freckles that rest gently, like honeydew
And the way that you scrunch up your nose when you laugh
Just confirms that you are going to be my better half

better half

11:11 make a wish
As if you don't know that my wish is this
You.
I wish for you to see me not see right through me
To view me as a person and not as the key
Used to unlock your own physical satisfaction
as i stare at the ceiling reviewing every single action
While you're snoring by my side out cold from the deed
Drowning out the sound that my mind and thoughts bleed
Telling me that i can be more to you in time
Because the best views come after the hardest climb
After all i am here to play the long game
But you lit the match and set my heart aflame
I want you right now
But you still insist somehow
That you are not ready for a relationship in general
If you were you'd choose me not any other girl and trust
there's several
People that would apparently fall to their knees for you
But i stand here loyal and yet you can't catch a clue
And trust me i'm terrified to hand to you my heart
But that fear hasn't stopped me and it's not about to start
instead i look at you and smile as 11:12 appears on the clock
You ask what was my wish as our eyes begin to lock
I laugh a little and joke it was nothing at all
But I know that one day you soon will begin to fall

11:11

Love is a choice
But you choosing not to love
Won't silence the voice

choice is yours

You squeeze the air
Right out of my lungs
Weighing heavy on my chest
Like one-hundred-thousand tons

Breathless

i want to go home
not to four walls and a welcome mat
home to you
your arms
your smile
your gentle kiss on my forehead
your warm embrace
you

I have had so many people tell me not to waste my time
That the idea of you is too good to be true and you will never
fully be mine
But i can't help but hold on to any last piece of you that i have
left
Cause letting you walk away would be ripping my heart out of
my chest

Holding On

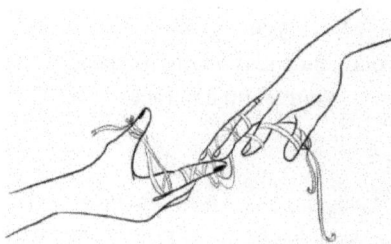

All i want is for you to stay
I could be in the darkest tunnel and your presence would light
the way
You bring a new light that i have never seen before
And it's one that i cannot wait to simply explore

stay

How much longer am i going to let this go on
Any sense of clarity has already been so far gone
It has been months of my life that i've given to you
And i still have no idea, not even a clue
As to what we are if there is anything at all
And I know it's quite obvious that i have already begun to fall
And when i do i fall fast and i fall hard
But the barrier is up and i can't let down my guard
Because i'm scared to be hurt by someone that i care so much
about
And a part of me loves you without a shadow of a doubt
But the other part tells me that my heart is going to break
When the dream fades to nightmare and i'm shaken awake
So when is the right time to lay my heart on the line
I just hope all the bads in my head and all the stars are aligned

dream fades to nightmare

I know that i fall hard and a little too fast
typically for the people that i know will never last
and i may not always be the most right
but if things ever crumble,
i will put up a good fight

worth the fight

I am so lost even myself is confused
And the last thing i want is for her to feel used
And i want to give her everything that she longs for
But i am scared love will come knocking at my door
I don't think im ready to trust her with my heart
The last one ended so bad i tell myself to act smart
But each time i stare into her eyes of blue
It makes me question everything that i thought i already knew
She cares for me deeper than anyone has before
She provides a sense of security like caring for me isn't a
chore
And i love how easy it is to talk to her for hours
Her smile is contagious like it contains super powers
But i can't let myself fall in love with her
No strings attached is simply what i prefer
Even though time stops when we are together
And i wish i could simply look at her forever
But her eyes ask a question she so desperately wants to know
Will i keep leading her on, commit, or finally let her go
And i don't even know the answer, i wish that i did
But breaking her heart is something that i simply forbid
Because whether i want to or not i care for her deeply
And I want to let myself just dive in completely
But i jump back and forth between questioning and knowing
And until i know completely the winds of uncertainty will
continue blowing

from his perspective

Baby i have you
And i won't let you go
I know this feeling is new
But you deserved it long ago

new but deserved

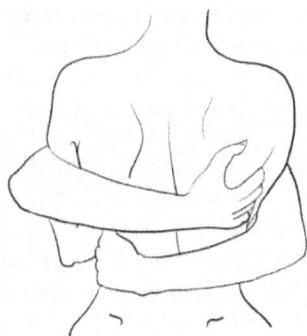

Will you be my...
Yes
I don't care what we are i just want you in my life
Whether i am you friend, your girlfriend, partner in crime, or
your wife
I don't think you understand how much you mean to me
I just want you by my side, in your eyes my future i see
So yes i'll be your friend
If that's what you need, together till the end
Or yes i'll be your girlfriend
Our lives together can begin to blend
And if a partner in crime is what you need
Then that's what i'll be as you already make my heart bleed
But if you ask me to marry you and to be your wife
Just know that i've been ready for this moment my entire life

I will be your...

This is your reminder
That we are now a two man team
So fighting each battle together
Should without a doubt be our theme

team of two

You make me speechless
Like the words flooding from my mouth are somehow
meaningless
Even though you listen and never make me feel unheard
You might think what i have to say is actually absurd
Did i get the wrong idea on what we are doing
Did i mistake your friendliness as romantic pursuing
But at any time you could have chosen to walk away from me
Leave me in the dust to never again have to see
But something about me keeps you around
I've lost my footing for you have shaken the ground
And to me my path is obvious and straight
It leads right to you i'd never make you wait
But yours is more complicated, crooked if you will
But you have to find the way on your own, it isn't something i
can instill

speechless

They say when you love somebody let them go
But i think it should be if you love them you need to let them know
Life changes paths in the blink of an eye
And love turns to hate but i really don't understand why
How can someone's second half, their best friend, their lover
Become someone they loathe, they don't recognize, change their
colors
And somehow both sides leave a relationship saying
They were too good for them while the other was playing
But two people can't both be the good guy
One had to be better and the other one has to lie
But still how can one go from dying to see someone
To never wanting to speak to them again, to being undeniably done
People say they love everything about their partner, even their flaws
And yet when it's over they despise what they used to applaud
The blue eyes they used to see their future in turned gray
And when their paths cross in public they choose to look the other
way
The smile that once was so contagious doesn't spread across their
face anymore
And every red flag that was brushed under the rug they now cannot
ignore
And the inside jokes that only the two knew
Are now forbidden words that both just want to undo
The hundreds of memories made and pictures taken are erased and
deleted
Both sides are leaving the relationship horribly defeated
Because the person they thought they were going to tie the knot with
and stand by their side
Has now taken the rope and the knot is undeniably untied
And it's hard to think that this is going to happen to me
But i guess heartbreak is the cost because love isn't free
but everytime im about to hand my heart to someone new
Im genuinely scared for what its about to go through

cost of love

Heartbreak

I don't think that i believe in love anymore
I always thought i was a hopeless romantic but that was before
I heard the way men talk about girls behind their backs
Like we're simply objects to help them reach their own climax
And i know you can't put every guy into this category
Love is a book and everyone gets to write their own story
But i haven't met many who can prove this theory wrong
So i convince myself there isn't someone who will simply
come along
And be the prince charming that i have always dreamed of
meeting
a lifeline for me, someone who keeps my own heart beating
Because each time i think that i actually love someone
Their true intentions become clear and make me want to be
done
Believing in something whose first word is literally hopeless
Love means nothing to me now even though it hurts to
confess

I don't believe in love anymore

I think i hate you
I hate you for everything that you just put me through
All the mental pain, the overthinking,
the physically feeling my heart get ripped out of my chest
while you're out there living
I hate you for making me only see the good
For believing that my feelings for you were nothing but
understood
I hate you for making me want to hate you
For convincing myself that with you my own love of life grew
I hate you for taking it all back
For thinking that you could just return my heart the farthest
thing from intact
I hate that you don't see where you went wrong
Playing me, using me, dragging me all along
To be there when you need me but never the other way around
And then tossed aside when newer and better was all of a
sudden found
I hate you for what what you did to me
But at least now i can move on from you because i'm setting
my own heart free

hate

I've always been considered to be quite outspoken
A defense mechanism for fear of being broken
But for some reason i can't find the words with you
I open my mouth and yet nothing will come through
And it's not because i simply have nothing to say
But because i'm terrified my words will scare you away
I know what i want and more importantly what i need
And i overthink every situation making my own mind bleed
Because you give me all that i long for
But outweighing my wants, i don't want to lose you even more

losing you

I got down on my literal knees for you
And not in a sexual way, if only you knew
When i dropped to my knees my hands clasped together
And i prayed, to God, that you could withstand this stormy
weather
I haven't turned to Him in way too fucking long
But why is it you that makes me pray again doesn't that seem
wrong
That the only thing that made me cry out for him again
Was the thought of me losing you now i just can't comprehend
I sobbed for you until my own stomach hurt
waited for your name to light up my phone in alarming yet
relieving alert
Asked your friends about you to make sure you were even
alive
Hoped that out of the darkness of ghosting you would
suddenly arrive
And hold me, and love me, tell me you're here and here to
stay
That you will never permanently turn your back on me and
walk through the doorway
But instead all of my prayers were never heard or understood
Because even God knew that us together is not undeniably
good

down on my Knees

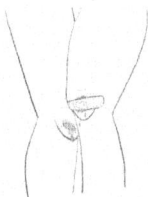

Nobody is ready to love me the right way
And in avoiding heartbreak they never choose to stay
nobody wants the guilt of shattering the heart
Of someone who deserves the world not just being your spare
part

loving the right way

You weren't there
when i needed you the most
I needed your arms around me
But i didn't even have your ghost

ghost

We are only as strong
As our weakest moment in time
If we can't help each other through it
Life will be an endless climb

the climb

You know those friends that you become strangely close with really fast
But something in your heart tells you that there's no chance it will last
Because the entire thing was simply too good to be true
and this person is now someone who knows everything you've ever gone through
but this fact isn't bad in and of itself
It's almost like the pain of putting a good book back on the shelf
except the pages are now torn and some are even missing
Just like a part of yourself is regretfully wishing
That you never opened up to them in the first place
As they now know too much and it is backfiring in your face
You put too much in and it took too much out of you
People told you that it's one sided and now you're finally seeing that it's true
But the act of leaving seems harder than staying
Because you have to admit that the thought of losing them is weighing
Heavily down on your mind and your heart
Even though that you know you guys are better apart
It felt as if you were fighting for something they never thought worth fighting for
They put in the bare minimum and you always put in more
And this toxicity undeniably went both ways
Neither were good for the other and yet both have always stayed
Everything's a competition, and words tore each other down
Things indirectly said would trigger the breakdowns
And it felt like every single day you were walking on eggshells
And i hate to say it but maybe it's time for the farewells
Because it's not eggshells anymore it's broken glass
And the cuts on your feet are signs that this is not going to just pass
Some people are simply just not compatible or meant to be friends
They saying is literally all good things must come to an end
Everything seems to have an underlying motive or reasoning
Because they come out stronger, from my weakening
Opinions start to differ solely to not agree
And people on the outside start to tell you what they see
Because they know that you deserve better
But they'll indirectly tell you maybe send a text or a letter
Because you need to come to the conclusion on your own
That this friendship is harmful and this person is no longer your home
So as you take another step along the shattered glass on the floor
You are walking away from the hurt, the blood, and more
And I promise i know that you are in agonizing pain
But losing this one person opens the door for so many others to gain
The wonderful, selfless, deserving girl that you are
That you won't even notice the bloodied cuts have faded to a scar
And this scar will never leave as it acts as a lesson
For every toxic relationship has made its lasting impression
But it has led you to happiness and genuine friendships you see loud and clear
And the broken glass along the floor was just a path leading you here

Walking on glass

Your hands were cold to the touch
There was no warmth inside you to find and clutch
Your eyes were glossy and blank
You had no soul inside you like your boat has already sank
Your mouth was on a mission that nobody could stop
The force behind your kiss instantly made my heart drop
Your ears were shut off to the world around you
If you could hear you would have heard from my mouth the
word no spew
Your legs were stronger than any force that i have known
My body was trapped, i shouldn't have come, i should've
known
Your arms were aggressive, each touch left a mark
A good person in the light, a monster in the dark
My vision was blurred from the tears in my eyes
I cannot break free of you despite my best tries
My mouth is frozen no words will fall out
Voice has disappeared from all the no's i had to shout
My ears are still ringing from the fight that i endured
And yet my mind still fails me, never able to be reassured
My legs are numb, in pain, and weak
I don't want to look down, i can't even take a slight peak
My arms are bruised from the force laid upon them
I used to be a flower, but you just broke the stem
You will forever be implanted in the back of my mind
Like a permanent branding that you have just signed

branding

Nobody talks about the heartbreak in watching someone else's
heartbreak
And i understand that their pain isn't mine to take
But i would volunteer my heart if it would save theirs
They deserve to know that someone out there cares
and watching as the color in their eyes fades to gray
i wish that i could take all of their brokenness away
Because I know i can put my own pieces back together
But i won't leave someone else alone to do theirs, no not ever
watching someone else's heartbreak is a different type of
broken
One that you can't pay to fix for its not a game that takes a
token

heartbreak in heartbreak

I don't do casual very well
And this isn't about what i wear or how i act if you can't
already tell
I can't do the no strings attached type thing
A casual hookup or an emotionless fling
I can't help but feel emotion towards that someone
And maybe we shared an intimacy that i felt a lot of and you
felt none
But either way i can't just keep giving a piece of me to you
Without noticing my feelings towards you have obviously
grew
I start to care for someone more than they care for me
And they tend to prey on my emotions because they know it is
the key
To keeping me around at the ring of their bell for their
pleasure
And as i begin to care for them i will take any measure
To guarantee they know that i would drop everything for them
And deep down i know i wish they viewed me as a gem
But i am simply something to fuck late at night
When all other options fail and they know i'll always be in
sight
But after every time my thoughts grow more and more
intrusive
You will never give me what i want and that is to be exclusive
I am so used to being used for my body and my heart
Because no matter what you do, to me you are always set apart
And yeah i wonder why this happens to me so often
You would think that the continuous cycle would teach me to
proceed with caution
But i am waiting for the person to come into my life and stay
And until then i will try to do casual even if it sets my peace
astray

casual

why is it so hard to understand the word no
i tried to convince myself maybe you thought i say go
but i didn't and we both know it
and i'm still waiting for you to look at me and admit
that you took something from me that i wasn't ready to give
and i blocked that night out not ready to relive
you betraying my trust and the spot in my heart i had for you
and you probably don't even remember but i wish beyond that
you knew
you will forever be a thief in my mind
and you made me lose my lingering hope in all of mankind
i can't even tell my parents what you did
i can't break their hearts too, no that i forbid
because if any of us are going to come out of this broken
it's going to be me because i know i will rise and
never let you know that you had power over me
but because of you i am now a lock and you just stole the key

the word no

Our relationship is incompatible
Based on jealousy
Praying on each others downfall
Is no easy delicacy
But it is just one of the many offenses
That led me to put up a barrier of defenses

jealous delicacy

I am the secret
That must never be said
And if someone were to find out
The scissors will undoubtedly cut the thread

secret

I am alone again with this emotional feeling
What is it about me that is so unappealing
people just want to fuck me and leave
why is sticking around so hard to conceive
Am I too much, too loud, too committed, too bold?
I'm over here handing my heart to you to hold
yet you leave it barely beating on the floor
And i'm left wondering is love even worth it anymore

worth it anymore

Lusted by many loved by none
Words of Devou on hookup culture being the loaded gun
And no, you're not getting shot in a literal way
But each hookup adds up and begins to chip away
At self concept, self worth, and even self confidence
You begin to go numb, not care, lose your consciousness
Because although many may want you in a sexual sense
Being used for your body is at your hearts expense
Turn off your emotions don't get too attached
The empty feeling when it's over is one that is unmatched
For either you just used someone or they used you
For physical gratification i'm sorry but it's true
They probably don't even remember your name
But they'll text you tomorrow as they want your body to claim
Of course only in the late hours off the night
When the darkness has set and there is no sign of light
Because god forbid that light illuminates your face
if anyone finds out its you, you'll become the disgrace
And if you tell your friends it makes it too real
as word spreads like wildfire you will lose your appeal
They only want u as their own secret, a mystery, their sneaky link
Like a prize that has been won, you dubbed let me buy you a drink
Cheers, dap up ur friend another body added to the count
Whos gonna achieve the highest amount
Place a bet with your buddies whos gonna bed them
Lie to them, sweet talk them, call them a diamond no, a gem
But really they're a hole or something to stick in
It happens so fast and almost on a whim
9pm 10pm 11pm you send the text
Come slide, u up, i'm bored, lets sext
Ur not down, ur asleep, u don't respond, that's fine
Onto the next i promise there's someone else in line
No talking. No cuddling. Simply just fuck
Be safe. Use protection. Dont test ur luck
Cause who's to say they would even stick around
Besides the whole point of hooking up is to not be tied down
But hooking up is also good because it's so easy
And people typically refrain if it's something makes them uneasy
Because it can be fun, and wild, and freeing
Like ur playing a great game cause theres no refereeing
Or as if a broken guitar still plays a beautiful song
Because the strings aren't attached nothing can go wrong
And i'm not asking you to do it or to not
I am, however, asking to give it some thought
Between 60 and 80 percent of students report that yes
They have engaged in hookup culture and that's only people who confessed
So it's here, its hot, its spreading like wildfire
That can be summed up to lust, to longing, to desire

hookup culture

Pain

My mind has hurt more then just me
It's written on their faces how much i make them worry
And all i really wanted was to make them proud
But those voices in my head are screaming so loud
It's not their fault i wish that they knew
The blames all on me there's nothing they could do
But the pain in their eyes makes me hurt more
I just want to be normal is that too much to ask for
I wish i could be wrapped in a permanent hug
But something tells me my grave has already been dug

hurt more than me

Friends fight
No, honey, that's not right
Friends fight for you
They don't direct the fight at you

friends fight

Sometimes my mind torments me past what i can handle
A depression so deep it could start quite the scandal
I can only sit in distress for so long at a time
Before the only relief is to cause such a crime
To my very own body i know it's hard to understand
But sometimes physical pain takes away from the emotional
strand
I can focus on the discomfort and pinpoint why i am suffering
Instead of not knowing why im not okay and constantly
wondering
Why my brain is hardwired the way that it is
And each day that passes i sink further into the abyss
So feeling the sharpness brush up against my skin
Distracts from the real problem causing a temporary win
But as i watch the blood pool from the mark that i made
I realize the dangerous game that is now being played
Because i get addicted to any diversion of the truth
And i am holding the very thing that just stole my youth
And once the temporary high bids its farewell
Im alone again in the darkness my own living hell

living hell

I don't want to be the girl in the mirror
Tears blur my vision every time that i see her
Who is the girl staring back at me
It sure isn't the person that i wanted to be

girl in the mirror

some people wonder why i put on a show
maybe if i cover every insecurity nobody will know
that deep down inside i'm a lock without a key
but if i put it all out there first it's not being stolen from me

stolen

From the moment i wake up in the morning to the time i fall asleep at night i
am lost
I wake up with the sun and based in the amount of warm rays i can feel
against my face through the windows i know how my day will go and how
much energy it will cost
I go through the same motions every morning to prepare me for the events of
the day
I stare at my reflection brushing my teeth telling myself maybe today will
finally go my way
I comb through my hair criticizing the way it falls around my face
Then try to scrub every flaw off of my skin because god forbid any
imperfections leave a trace
I gently blink the black paste of mascara through my lashes to highlight the
one feature that i don't hate
Leave before i stare for too long and the girl in the mirror begins to decide my
fate
I dress in baggy clothes believing that what people don't see they can't judge
me on
But the second night rolls around the clothes will drop from my shoulders and
all modesty is gone
I walk through campus with my eyes glued to the ground or glossed over
looking in front of me
Deep within my own thoughts looking but not registering anyone or anything
that i see
I go to class and i try, i listen and i study, and yet it is never enough
I leave every test telling myself to study harder and next time it won't be as
rough
My campus takes my breath away no matter the time of day
But somehow since coming here the vibrant colors have faded to gray
I think about the past a lot and can't help but want to go back
I never knew that being here alone would send my mind under attack
I want the comfort of living at home and having family waiting for me
Home cooked meals, family nights, and living each day carefree
I am so stuck in a routine that never fails to be the same
This place feels so small as if i know every player in the game
But i rather lose the game completely then to keep playing like this
Maybe the comfort of my past will return, but for now i just reminisce

lost

I never really understood why things would affect me so much
But people's words and actions place an everlasting touch
And no matter how badly i want to shake free of them
It's a forever type thing like you have already been condemned
A word causes more damage than any action could
And the words told to six year old me were the ones that stole
my childhood
Because they weren't in one ear and out the other
They stayed put inside my head to linger and to bother
I hated myself due to what others told me
And the words they used to describe me were what i began to
see
And once i believed them there was no going back
Because little did i know those words would have such an
impact
I wanted to fit the mold of what everyone saw as perfect
But chasing this image has had a lasting effect

the impact

I can't look in the mirror without tearing myself apart anymore
And i hate every part of me even the ones i used to adore
I know i didn't deserve all of this as a child
But come on, let's be honest, a words impact is wild

torn apart

Each day that goes on i'm convinced more and more that I am the most
irrational person
Whether it be in my personal, social, or academic life i can't help but watch it
worsen
I was told tonight by a guy that I have a very cute vibe
But in the same night a girl told me that rbf was my only trait to describe
I've been told that I am the sweetest person in the room to i'm nothing but a
bitch
And most of the time it doesn't bother me, but sometimes these words make
my people-pleasing side itch
I place too much value on words that float freely in the air
My night gets ruined too easily by things that I shouldn't give a second care
I'm a really good observer, i tend to stay to myself in the back
Because if people never see me then they won't notice all the things i also lack
I remember a lot of things specifically important stories and dates
And sometimes a little more random like knowing people's license plates
I watch people from afar and can pick up on the little things with ease
I believe if i remain silent i won't give into toxicities disease
But when im quiet and alone in the back of the room
It leaves room in my head to for thoughts to roam, to plant, and to bloom
but beauty doesn't sprout from my mind
But rather weeds that spread and grow simply to find
Every ounce of myself that doubts the rest
And it holds me to silence unable to speak as if my voice is on house arrest
And all this goes on while im sitting quietly alone
And trust me the fact that it isn't rational is a fact that i have known
I feel like i'm going more insane every time that i blink my eyes
Like i am stuck in a bubble while the time around me flies
I fight back tears that desperately want to stain my cheeks too often
And i tell myself if these people gave me a chance my thick exterior would
soon soften
But people like to judge before they know what's beneath the surface
Maybe getting to know me makes them undeniably nervous
But really i think people gravitate towards what is easy and clear
But everyday i wake up with less desire to being here
And i don't mean that i simply want to die
But moreover i want to skip this part where i feel i am waiting for my actual
life on standby
I'm tired of waking up not wanting to be where i am
Not knowing who i am aside from the VEA monogram
And these are just some reasons why i think im as irrational as can be
In all honesty this poem was supposed to be about the happy go lucky me

no rationale

Crimson stains down my sleeve
Body numb
I'm ready to leave

TW

I smile wide
For you to see
A smile so big
It fools even me
I laugh often
For you to hear
A laugh so loud
Your smile will appear
I cry at night
For no one can know
A cry so painful
It stole my glow

stolen

I will sit alone in the darkness
Staring at what's causing my pain
And as I don't even understand it
It's even more impossible to explain

can't understand, can't explain

I wish i could count how many tears i have let fall for you
But the countless amount is not something i can undo
My cheeks are now left with a permanent stain
I wish someone warned me that with love comes pain

love comes pain

Sometimes i wonder why i can only write about the darkness
and the pain
But i think it's because every moment in my life has left a
noticeable stain
And the good easily washes away but the bad is all that i
remember
The warmth of summer is temporary and the rest is as cold as
december

cold

toxicity courses through my blood
and i don't necessarily project it
but rather attract the flood

flood

My biggest fear Is that of my own body
If i don't look a certain way how will i ever be somebody
The gap between my thighs isn't big enough
My defined muscles have faded, i no longer look tough
My fingers can only reach around my forearm so high
Sucking in doesn't make a difference no matter how hard i try
My double chin makes its appearance when i least want it to
It stands out in pictures and just when i thought my confidence
grew
i am humbled once again by the reflection staring back at me
unbreakable eye contact and yet i don't recognize what i see

body

blonde and blue
my only value

me

I'm familiar with the feeling of just wanting to cry
digging into my thoughts just to figure out why
But i can't quite figure it out
So my mind drifts away as i continue to doubt
Why can't I be alone ?
And not in the single and ready to mingle zone
I mean alone in a room simply by myself
Single is one thing, but me, singular a different stealth

single vs singular

i am underwater
Screaming at the top of my lungs
But my voice is drowned out
By the thousands of tons
Of water pulling me down
Far away from life's bliss
It's okay i've been falling for years
I'm not new to the abyss

drowning

I am so sorry for believing your smile
And not noticing as the weights on your shoulders piled
I wish that i could have taken away all of your pain
But it's too late, i failed, until we meet again

until we meet again

the silence of the room is growing more loud
As you realize you are alone in navigating this crowd
So you retreat back to the depths of your mind
Seeking some comfort but only to find
A compartment of thoughts that won't quiet down
As you beg that your mind just becomes a ghost town

ghost town

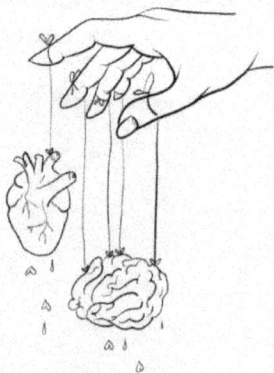

My thoughts are racing
My heart is aching
A piece of me has been slowly breaking
From the stress and the pressure
Of being enough
Don't show your pain
You've got to act tough
Because god forbid that something is actually wrong
With the girl that they've raised
to always be strong

racing, aching, breaking

An outsider
In my own body and mind
And i cannot change it
It's just how i'm designed

outsider

When is it going to be my turn
I have learned enough
Healed enough
And now it's starting to burn

my turn

Why am i the one always being used
For my body and my heart
I am quite confused
Hurting me gets you nowhere
But still you left me alone, gasping for air

breathless

I can't walk away
From what's causing my fight
Like i'm too close to the fire
But am mesmerized by the light

mesmerized

Social media tells me
Exactly how to look
And i was confident
That would never be my hook
But little did i know
Ed would be writing my book

the look, the hook, the book

I have lost my sight
The end of the tunnel has disappeared
I can no longer see the light
Nothing is guiding me through life anymore
My feet are now glued to rock bottoms cold floor

rock bottom

I know you don't believe the smile on my face but rather the
pain in my eyes
You always listen to what i'm willing to share and have never
been one to pry
But you are the only one to notice that the sorrow behind my
eyes falls deep
the hurt runs like blood, filling, overflowing, and now it's
beginning to seep
Looking at you seeing my pain fills my own eyes with tears
I can't watch my hurt, hurt you i can handle it alone i've done
it for years
My brokenness shouldn't break you too
It's the last thing i want for you to go through

running deep

my pain is not for me but for you
i wish there was a way to take the weight of everything you've
gone through
and add the pain to my shoulders to relieve yours
knowing that my love for you is what undoubtedly endures
because i will walk through any fire to make sure you don't
burn
and knowing you're okay is all i need in return

burn for you

No one ever sticks around
To help me swim when i want to drown
They always leave when things get hard
Like my pain is easy to simply disregard

disregarded

I feel everything all at once
And yet nothing at all
Almost like i've stopped moving forward
And am stuck behind a brick wall

all at once

What if i told you my best friends name was ed
Some might think he's imaginary or only lives in my head
But he made his appearance in the real world long ago
And trust me his life here has been quite the show
He taught me how to hate every inch of myself
To put every ounce of self love back up on the shelf
Because only self destructive thoughts were allowed to be had
And none of these thoughts were able to be considered bad
He showed me what a calorie was and how to count
How many i could have in a day a very specific amount
I learned how to dodge concerned comments or questions
And ignored all acts of help or any minor suggestions
Because the only teacher i could listen to went by the name of
ed
And oftentimes i would react to his lessons with dread
What if i don't want to throw up every meal
My bodies tired and in pain i want out of this deal

best friend named ed

Sometimes i feel like
I'm too far gone
My grip is beginning to slip
I can no longer hold on

too far gone

I am stuck
As if at 20 my mid life crisis has already struck
Life is a routine that is the same thing every day
There is no color to the world just a whole lot of gray
And i try to explain this feeling to those around me
But they never quite understand even though every ounce of
me is pleading
Because i'm sinking fast into the depths of quicksand
And i'm reaching with everything to grab onto someone's
hand
But there's no one there to simply help me out
So I remain stuck, wondering if this is what life's all about

stuck

i am more than my body and my weight
and this is something i have never been able to actually restate
because i'm told it on repeat by the people that love me
but i simply cannot allow my own eyes to see
the strength and the beauty that my body holds
because i want one thing while a different story unfolds
and i've taken things into my own hands many times before
and it has left me lifeless and broken lying on the floor
but once rock bottom has fully been met
i say a new start has begun and a new tide has been set
but in the back of my mind my old habits rest
if self love is the topic i will never pass the test

the topic of self love

Moving On

We may not be in love anymore but i will always love you
We shared a connectedness that only we knew
and that doesn't disappear the moment we say its over
not letting myself hate you is what gives me my closure
so whether or not things ended on a good or bad note
There was a time where you were the only thing keeping me
afloat
So i will forever be grateful for the support that you gave me
We had a genuine love and i hope that you agree
But now we must move on to bigger and better
And this poem can act as my final goodbye letter

goodbye

Sometimes i wonder what i ever saw in you
I manifested us for so long if only you knew
But it's crazy to see how much of it i regret
And based on how much we both put in you are in a major
debt
Because i gave everything that i had
While you withheld most for fear it would end bad
I guess you were right things did ultimately end
And the moment they did my heart was already on the mend
Because you lost something much greater than you
And i was finally understanding that what my mom told me
was true
You were realizing everything that you had lost
And i was seeing the only thing you did for me was exhaust
So while i'm moving on to the furthest thing from you
You're still caught up on the girl you once knew

the girl you once knew

Hey baby girl
The world is at your feet
It's not time to throw in the towel
And to accept your defeat

it's not time

Not knowing is exhausting i'm starting to lose all hope
On actually being something with you i guess it's how i cope
Truly being seen by someone isn't a lot to ask for
I know because it's the bare minimum and i deserve much
more
Call it what you want but i need to move on
Even though i'm trying to convince myself what we had isn't
gone

Magic doesn't fade in the blink of an eye
Everything has a process but i wish ours didn't end with
goodbye

notice me

I wonder what it's going to be like when i go to heaven
Will angels be singing or will i enter to tunes on a violin
Is it going to be so bright
that i have to shield my eyes from being blinded by the light
Is it going to feel like home?
Because i honestly don't know what that feels like anymore
i'm so used to being alone
I catch myself daydreaming of leaving this place
As the obstacles are increasingly difficult to stand up and face
And i know 20 is to young to simply just leave
My time isn't up there is more i need to achieve
But i never really realized how much i dreaded being alive
Each day is the same and i feel like i've lost all of my drive
But is heaven the answer to all of this
Cause in my head i picture perfection, serenity, and bliss
But in reality nobody i love is even there
Instead they are here, living and breathing earthly air
It's not my time to go and that's simply that
I just have to figure out how to not be life's little doormat

Heaven

Someday
i will be somebody's first choice
Where i don't have to shout
For them to hear my voice

someday

All i wanted
Was for your name to pop up on my phone
Even if no words were said i wanted to know that you thought
about me
Even if it was for just a second
But no
Your name didn't show up
And i was left sitting there going through the motions of life
overthinking every single thing about you and me
I wasn't on your mind
And yet you were the one thing that never left mine
You lingered
As if someone who was uninvited but didn't get the memo to
leave
But even though you didn't reach out and i was finally
beginning to move on
To not count on you, to not let you have any affect on my days
I still had a last sliver of hope in the back of my mind and
depths of my heart that you would out of nowhere show up
And then it did
When i least expected and finally convinced myself that i
didn't want it there it was
Your name lighting up my phone
My heart skipped a beat or maybe even two
I stared at it until the phone went dark
You were all i wanted
But you are nothing that i need

all i wanted

Boredom is taken for granted
In the silence
A seed of thought planted

Some people come
Into your life
For a reason
And some people
Only stay briefly,
Just for a season

a reason, or a season

People's response to me showing any emotion, good or bad, is
to ask "have you written about it"
And although it is my usual outlet sometimes not all of my
feelings fit
Into a colorful rhyme expressing all of my doubt
Sometimes i need to talk it through to find my own paths next
route

talk

Once again i'm left alone in my room
wondering why
I'm staring at my phone
awaiting your reply
Because if you wanted to you would
it's not that complicated
I want to be prioritized
not just tolerated

tolerated

I have big dreams and yet i don't know what they are
Because starting my "real life" still seems so far
And i know it will come with the blink of an eye
But i'm scared of failure so i rather just not try
I have a hard time picturing my future like
Will i find love, have a family, or have a job i dislike
I don't want to find out the world is as disappointing as i
assume
A repeating cycle until you meet your tomb
And once i decide what my life is going to be
It's too permanent a decision and i know i will never be
Content with the same thing over and over
No luck at all where's the four leaf clover
So i choose to stay with my future being a mystery
Because maybe then i'll become something or even go down
in history

down in history

I want you
I need you
I loved you
I lost you
I miss you
I regret you

you

I find the most comfort in the darkness
Like somehow every worry disappears into the starkness
But really in reality its when im the most deep in thought
In tune with my mind and narrowing down the things i can fix
and the things i cannot
The darkness brings a peace that the light simply eliminates
And through the silence my mind is no longer waiting at, but
walking through the gates
To sitting with my emotions rather than running from them in
fear
Scared of letting all the pain in and maybe even being told
what i don't want to hear
But i'm writing this in complete, and utter darkness
Listening to the rain, emotions flooding, tears drop against my
cheek with a gente kiss
Because in the darkness i get a subtle glimpse of all life's bliss

darkness is bliss

i don't know how i'm going to move on from you
my love is stronger than ever holding me to you
like glue
but in the loudness of my falling your silence drowned out the
noise
acting like love is the enemy and letting it in only destroys
but so much is being said through no words at all
but you were a drug and i'm in the peak of withdrawal

drug

I would love you with everything that i've got
But if you can't do the same for me
Is that love something that I actually want?

is it worth it

I have an overwhelming desire
To go back to when i was a child
Where my life was so pure
And my personality wild

pure and wild

is it someone's job to save their friend from loving someone
who doesn't deserve it
because picture them as fire and you're blowing out the flame
that you have fought to keep lit
is it worth it to hurt them sooner rather than later
knowing that undeserving love is the ultimate traitor
or is it a friends job to hold their tongue
not point out the bee until they've already been stung
be there to hold them when the heartbreak stings and the fire
burns
make sure the light in their eyes undoubtedly returns
or is it your job to break their heart first
shatter the pieces and watch as they disperse
then pick them back up one piece at a time
hold their hand and guide them through the unimaginable
climb
i honestly don't know which is the job of a friend
i guess it's to each their own and all just depends

the job of a friend

a mother should never have to bury their own child
i understood the saying before the weights on my shoulders
piled
but being six feet below the ground seemed like the only
choice
that would make the pain end and silence the voice
that's ringing in my head telling me that it's my time to go
but i can't do that to my parents how will they ever know
that nothing they could've done would have stopped me
this was the only way to finally set my mind free
from the torment and demons that rest on my shoulder
and each and every day they grew a little more bolder
And i just hope my leaving won't kill them too
because their lives are still worth living but mine i can't undo

bury a child

I gave ed the middle finger almost four months ago
But this victory is only celebrated by me because nobody else
really knows
And if they do they don't know to the extent to which i am
proud
It's probably what i'm most proud of myself for and its surreal
to say out loud
I fought for this moment for so many years
And looking back I can almost say it was worth all of the
tears
I did it, i flipped the switch all on my own
I took a leap of faith straight into the unknown
I can't remember the last time ed didn't rule my life
It has been over six years of him dangling his sharp knife
Over my head in control of everything that i did
And i listened to what he told me to do and what he forbid
But i broke free of all of his bonds
And although i still occasionally hear his voice in my head i
no longer respond
Because fuck you ed once and for all
the scene is now over, take a bow, its your last curtain call

F U E.D.

I remember when tears stained my cheeks every day and every night
When life was full of only darkness and i didn't believe in any light
I remember when i would sit in my car and scream
My forehead hitting the steering wheel while all my anger and
sadness would stream
I remember when i wouldn't allow myself to eat
I craved the emptiness and the hunger, i found it almost sweet
I remember when i would sit on my bathroom floor
Not afraid that anyone would come walking through my door
And see me there with a piece of glass in my hand
Blood pouring from the mark i just made at the devil on my shoulders
command
I remember when i would stare in the mirror for hours
Or in attempt to feel something i would take scorching hot showers
I remember when my entire relationship with my parents was built
upon lies
When they knew i was in pain but yet i couldn't look them in the
eyes
I remember when all i wanted was to make them proud
But reality hit and i was torn away from my soft seat upon a cloud
I remember when after every meal i would drop to my knees
And i would beg over and over please come up with ease
I remember when i couldn't allow myself a full meal
I was afraid of every food, ed convinced me calories weren't part of
our deal
I remember when a number controlled my every day
What i consumed, what i burned, what i did depended on how much i
would weigh
I remember when i didn't want to alive anymore
When the thought of living seemed like the most dreaded chore
I remember when i would stay up all night trying
To convince myself that the answer to my pain wasn't dying

I remember

You are alive
Let the rain hit your face
And begin to revive
For the clouds have now parted
You are no longer deprived
Of what you need to stand tall, stand strong, and to thrive
For you were created to do more
More than just simply survive

alive

I like you too much to be okay
With you getting with other people i can't just look away
Because i have allowed for myself to fall
I know, not smart, i didn't learn at all
But i know that i can love you the right way
But if you can't do the same i can no longer stay
And my feelings won't fade
For a solid amount of time
But i cannot keep killing my heart
I've got to put an end to that crime

crime

What would I say if you asked if we could start over?
Its difficult because a part of me has wished for this moment
every four leaf clover
But to be completely honest and blunt with you
I would most likely say no because the pain isn't something
you can just undo
And no matter how hard my heart wants me to start fresh
Your words and your actions have left a permanent scar on my
flesh

scar

I don't want to give you my heart
Because what if falling for you makes it all fall apart
I'm finally content with it being just me
But deep down i know i want to dive in and see
What possibilities are in store if i went from one to two
And it terrifies me to start something knew
As my heart was shattered, i'm not sure how much more
It can take cause i alone picked the pieces up off the floor
I put the pieces back together but some are still missing
And i understand a part of me is damaged far beyond fixing
But i won't let the fear of being hurt again stop me
Cause each little shatter is the cost because love is not free
So here i am handing my heart to you to decide
Will you hold it tightly or toss it aside

falling apart

Today i started crying while i was alone in the car
But they weren't tears of sadness so it felt quite bizarre
And i didn't really understand why emotions were flooding in
But for the first time in forever i lifted up my own chin
I was crying tears of joy and of pure contentment
For i was finally living a life fully by my own consent
I have been listening to my heart and following my own needs
Letting the happiness in my mind wander and begin to plant
its seeds
To the rest of my life im sorry but i can't help but smile
This is the feeling i've been waiting for for more than just a
little while

contentment

They say that you attract what you are used to
But i want a love that is the furthest thing from you
I handed to you my heart and you held it for a little while
And in the beginning simply your presence always made me
smile
But then your grip on my heart grew even more tight
And the look in your eyes should have triggered fight or flight
But i stuck around convinced that i loved you
And i wanted to help you face all that you went through
But you threw my heart down onto the floor
And the pieces that shattered you viewed as a score
Cause the words tearing a piece of me each time that they
were said
Gave you a power that went straight to you head
You knew that i cared about what you thought of me
You manipulated me. Hurt me. Made me unable to flee
And when i finally thought i got away from the devil that you
are
I realized you lingered like an unhealing scar
And each person i have met and thought was good
Has reminded me of you and at first i misunderstood
But now i know that you set the stage
But this is MY book and i am choosing to turn the page

turning the page

Navigating life as a teenage girl is far from easy. This book follows the journey that I experienced while learning and growing through depression, body image issues, and various forms of eating disorders. All of which have played a major role in my growing up. I have also been learning about love, heartbreak, pain, and the beautiful art of moving on. Each journey is unique and no one journey is easy, but it is my hope that someone out there can relate to at least one of my poems. Here's to the last few years, through my eyes.

Description

Special thanks to my parents for supporting me through every challenge or obstacle thrown my way.

My friends for witnessing and processing these emotions with me and for believing in the power of words.

My therapist for encouraging me to write and to never stop.

My AP language teacher for not only giving me the knowledge to write, but even more so the love for it.

My beautiful cousin for creating the beautiful cover art and my good friend for illustrating the book. They truly made my vision come to life!

From the bottom of my heart, thank you

www.ingramcontent.com/pod-product-compliance
Lightning Source LLC
Chambersburg PA
CBHW021149090426
42740CB00008B/1010